Published in the United States by North-South Books Inc., New York

Published simultaneously in Great Britain, Canada,
Australia and New Zealand by North-South Books,
an imprint of Nord-Süd Verlag AG, Gossau Zürich, Switzerland.

Library of Congress Cataloging-in-Publication Data
Manson, Christopher.
A Farmyard song : an old rhyme with new pictures / Christopher Manson.
Summary: A cumulative rhyme in which various farm animals make appropriate
noises after being fed: cat goes fiddle-i-fee and pig goes griffy, gruffy.
ISBN 1-55858-169-3 (Trade binding)
ISBN 1-55858-170-7 (Library binding)
1. Nursery rhymes. 2. Children's poetry.
[1. Nursery rhymes. 2. Animal sounds—Poetry.] I. Title.
PZ8.3.M3563Far 1992
398.8—dc20   91-46238

A CIP catalogue record for this book is available
from The British Library

1 3 5 7 9 10 8 6 4 2
Printed in Belgium

*The illustrations in this book are*
*woodcuts painted with watercolor. The border*
*designs and decorative vignettes are*
*stenciled with watercolor.*

# A Farmyard Song

### An Old Rhyme
### with New Pictures by

## Christopher Manson

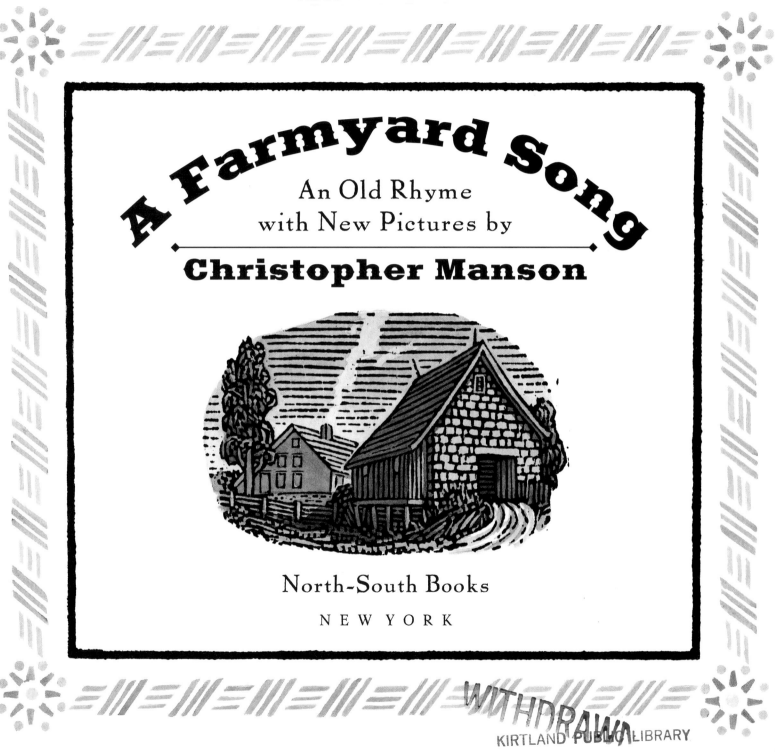

### North-South Books

### NEW YORK

I had a cat and the cat pleased me,
I fed my cat by yonder tree;
Cat goes fiddle-i-fee.

I had a hen and the hen pleased me,
I fed my hen by yonder tree;
Hen goes chimmy-chuck, chimmy-chuck,
Cat goes fiddle-i-fee.

I had a duck and the duck pleased me,
I fed my duck by yonder tree;
Duck goes quack, quack,
Hen goes chimmy-chuck, chimmy-chuck,
Cat goes fiddle-i-fee.

I had a goose and the goose pleased me,
I fed my goose by yonder tree;
Goose goes swishy, swashy,
Duck goes quack, quack,
Hen goes chimmy-chuck, chimmy-chuck,
Cat goes fiddle-i-fee.

I had a sheep and the sheep pleased me,
I fed my sheep by yonder tree;
Sheep goes baa, baa,
Goose goes swishy, swashy,
Duck goes quack, quack,
Hen goes chimmy-chuck, chimmy-chuck,
Cat goes fiddle-i-fee.

I had a pig and the pig pleased me,
I fed my pig by yonder tree;
Pig goes griffy, gruffy,
Sheep goes baa, baa,
Goose goes swishy, swashy,
Duck goes quack, quack,
Hen goes chimmy-chuck, chimmy-chuck,
Cat goes fiddle-i-fee.

I had a cow and the cow pleased me,
I fed my cow by yonder tree;
Cow goes moo, moo,
Pig goes griffy, gruffy,
Sheep goes baa, baa,
Goose goes swishy, swashy,
Duck goes quack, quack,
Hen goes chimmy-chuck, chimmy-chuck,
Cat goes fiddle-i-fee.

I had a horse and the horse pleased me,
I fed my horse by yonder tree;
Horse goes neigh, neigh,
Cow goes moo, moo,
Pig goes griffy, gruffy,
Sheep goes baa, baa,
Goose goes swishy, swashy,
Duck goes quack, quack,
Hen goes chimmy-chuck, chimmy-chuck,
Cat goes fiddle-i-fee.

I had a dog and the dog pleased me,
I fed my dog by yonder tree;
Dog goes bow-wow, bow-wow,
Horse goes neigh, neigh,
Cow goes moo, moo,
Pig goes griffy, gruffy,
Sheep goes baa, baa,
Goose goes swishy, swashy,
Duck goes quack, quack,
Hen goes chimmy-chuck, chimmy-chuck,
Cat goes fiddle-i-fee!

Dog goes . . .        Horse goes . . .

Hen goes . . .    Cat goes . . .